BALLADS
THE CRADLE

1.

A Magneus

BALLADS
THE CRADLE

1.

CONTENTS

DEDICATION

In dedication to Abraham

INTRODUCTION

"Brotherhood" and *"calling peace"* are part of human nature. As we *"chase desires"*, the epic life of Abraham is a model for many, just as it was for generations in the ancient and recent past.

Abraham offers myths and mysteries, charms and challenges, fate and faith, action and passion. All in one.

BALLADS: THE CRADLE (the 1st volume of 5), like a rock ballad, takes us to another dimension with its rhymes and rhythms.

A Magneus

LINEAGE

ABRAHAM

Avraham Avinu,
Forefather Abraham,
good shepherd of many,
of Onegod, the only.
Ibrahim, al-Khalil,
Forefather Abraham,
good old friend of plenty,
of Onegod, the only.

Patriarch Abraham,
Cradleland's wanderer,
fatherhood, calling peace,
good stronghold holding each.
Forefather Abraham,
Holyland's wonderer,
brotherhood within reach,
Good Foothold holding each.

THE CRY

Great Ur with walls and sighs
longed for summer nights' hope:
The Cry, that torched the skies
bold from Amathlai's hold.
Floodland's fertile crescent
joyed the poignant boy,
Terah's agile pleasance
joined the buoyant joy.

"Son Abram! Uplift us
right up to Sky Mighty.
you're chosen to bring us
righteousness divinely.
Forever be happy
as Father of many,
and never be lonely
as Leader of plenty!"

CARING ONES

Urudu's riverways
gently nurtured broad banks,
Idigna's silver waves
gladly nourished lush lands;
light sea breeze danced before
tangled strands, hidden nests,
while Abram waited for
tender breasts, sweetened naps.

A gay gleam, not yet seen,
shined on blond hair brightly,
mid daydreams, so serene,
smiled on fond heir rightly,
among all searching for
the shepherd of belief,
above all yearning for
the herder of relief.

BLOSSOM

Dawn tickles, low sunrise

on harbours spanned bridges

caught merchants' slow surprise

on shipboards and ridges.

Galiots' mythic troves,

azure coasts' hectic gales,

chariots mystic loads

brought and told epic tales.

Morn twinkles, slick sunshine

on wide stones' tanned ledges

sought archpriests' quick uprise

on high thrones and henges.

Noblemen of wisdom

kept sacred for ages,

privileged old kingdom

forever engages.

TERRACED FIRELILY

Terraced Firelily,

lavender, rosemary,

dearest jasmine, daisy

barely turned rose merry,

yet shy hearts felt lonely

in disguise blamefully,

and cried hard remotely

to the skies shamefully.

Terah was worshipping
Mother Earth's whispering.
Sumer was welcoming
Father Sky's wakening:
storm clouds were passing,
gathered at darkening,
small sunbirds were trembling,
threatened. But heartening.

QUARANTINE

At Moonnight's quarantine
nightingales, nocturnal,
at Moonbright's tangerine
sang of glades, fraternal,
at Moonsight's self-esteem
of gods, fays, supernal,
at Moonlight's self-redeem
of ponds, wells, eternal.

Yet humans caught cattle

for relished rituals,

emboldened brute battles

of anguished animals,

awed ordeals, ovations

for festal funerals,

dark doom deals, donations

of bestial burials.

HEADING HOME

Terah was heading home,

to Cradle of Credo,

Harran's warm nesting dome,

to shelter tomorrow,

to last grebes overflown

the fast streams, overblown,

to vast peaks overthrown

the past dreams, overgrown,

to Nahor of Faithdome,

the father at Moonlow,

to Nannar of Skydome,

the Moongod at Moonlow,

to show son at Hollow

the moonpray'rs of shadow,

two bison at Hallow,

the moonpreys of shallow.

GREAT LINEAGE

He believed in Heaven

and Adam of courage,

pretty Eve in Eden

preparing the voyage,

in Noah of Great Flood

supporting all salvage,

in Son Shem of great blood

opposing sore savage.

Could Abram, as firstborn,

envision the passage,

firm bedrock of faithdom

to capture the message,

to safeguard the great flock

with merit from bondage,

to faithguard The Great God

with spirit and homage?

BINDINGS

TREASURE TROVES

Hundredfold were the troves –
Harran's yields, orchard groves,
deep in vaults, golden ores,
far at fields, vineyard slopes;
sizzling hot air mirage,
caravans, sun-hit folks,
cool bazaar, street melange,
long serais, moonlit loads.

Everyoung, neverold
worked in roles at all costs,
evermore as were told,
building stalls at all ports;
travelers from abroad,
million miles, million more,
farewellers on the roads,
thousand times, thousand more.

QUAINT ALLEYS

Quaint alleys, passages,

beehive - shaped cottages,

aged grapevines, vintages,

skylark songs, birdcages

admired fine jewels'

captivating essence,

inspired skilled jewelers'

mesmerizing presence.

Teasing smells, furnaces,

attesting warm dishes,

tempting wine, fragrances,

attracting folk dances

gilded in opulence

essential principles,

lifted self-confidence,

celestial canticles.

AT KIN'S NEST

Bent Nahor, the sanest,

raised Abram, the finest,

with kinfolks at home's nest

praised 'Kinson', the earnest,

on the quest with goods' crest,

the splendour of the past,

all the zest at moon's fest,

the grandeur, so he asked,

"Skies! We need your aidance
along your midnight track,
ply with deeds and guidance
beyond your dreamlike tact,
for better alliance
in Eden with no bars,
forever admittance
in Heaven with all stars."

CHASE OF DESIRE

'Belly Mound' at Haze
with standing stones in praise,
witty ground at Blaze
withstanding storms in grace,
were proud of Divine
with beliefs well defined,
were round and benign
with reliefs well-designed.

Oath preachers and reachers

at clusters of caverns,

path makers and takers

at lusters of lanterns

in trance with the choir

at days of bonfire,

made dance wild and dire

at chase of desire.

SORROW

Cold teardrops fell upon

lamented death-pillow,

on Nahor, on and on,

dearly loved good fellow;

"Earth below! Oh, no, no!"

wept the folk, the widow,

cried the vault, the meadow,

mourned the oak, the willow.

Hammurabi Warlord,

blue Babylon's shadow,

dipped in muddy ox-ford,

new echelon's shallow;

loyal dream he borrowed,

seeking greet with arrow,

royal scheme he followed,

meeting grieve and mellow.

TWILIGHT FIRELILY

Twilight Firelily,

lavender, rosemary,

midnight tulip, daisy

bloomed to turn rose merry;

lying hearts sighed deeply

in disguise blamefully,

crying hard and lonely

to the skies shamefully.

Terah was worshipping
Mother Earth's whispering.
Harran was welcoming
Father Sky's wakening:
tense clouds kept raining,
wrinkled at darkening,
sad sunbirds kept shaking,
sickened. Yet, heartening.

FLOURISHED

Still Terah embraced life -
Son Abram from The Cry,
sweet 'Nuna', his goodwife,
sole sweetheart, day and night;
was nourished by vespers'
fulfilling songs, rich rhymes,
and flourished together
with growing flock's midnights.

The next one's red hair flamed,

with virtues was he named,

as Nahor, as they prayed,

for values was he raised;

at last, Haran, the tamed,

the rascal, the upraised,

adored Harran, the famed,

the cradle, as he played.

TIGHT BINDINGS

"You rascals, my seedlings,

who tricks me at wrestling?",

sons replied with snuggling,

with giggle and hugging,

with daily appearings,

unbreakable bindings,

with daily appealings,

untearable tidings.

They satisfied idols

as if were paternal,

they sacrificed icons

as if were eternal,

while Nannar, wife Ningal

laughed and laughed like jackals,

while pure faith in Abram

swelled and swelled with chuckles!

PATHGUARDS

AGAINST ALL ODDS

Shop idols of Terah
sent night spells ruthfully
on Abram and Harran
with nightmares awfully:
angered boys balefully
amidst throes dreadfully
shattered dolls banefully
against odds vengefully.

Mad Nemrut, The Hunter,

set dungeon rapidly,

glad Abram, the hunted,

grabbed Haran hastily;

ran in dales playfully,

barren vales pridefully,

slept for days painfully,

dwelled in caves pray'rfully.

POWER OF FAITH

The rampage was brutal

at Urfa's cathedral

of Nemrut. The Royal,

at Abram's refusal:

Doom pillars damn' fatal

had sling-thrown the rascals

to embers of scandal

in torn rags and sandals.

Oh, what a miracle,

Sky transformed the trial

to Garden Magical,

to Fishpond Eternal,

and siblings at sunfall

examined The Sunglow,

"Who are you among all,

The True One Above All?"

WATER FIRELILY

Water Firelily,

lavender, rosemary,

floating lotus, daisy

gladly turned rose merry,

lightened hearts prettily,

in disguise gracefully

smiled and winked wittily

to the skies gratefully.

Abram was worshipping
Mother Earth's whispering.
Urfa was welcoming
Father Sky's wakening.
white clouds were gently
sleeping at darkening.
while sunbirds were sweetly
tweeting. Kept heartening.

MARCHINGS

Hammurabi's hunger

with strike of a tiger

captured father's honour

with bites of a viper,

so driven by order

enforced the takeover,

so drunken by power

enjoyed the hangover.

Stunned Terah in big shock

gathered men and livestock,

worn wagons, esteemed stocks,

stubborn mules and bullocks,

to cross choking charlocks,

to reach Ur's beloved blocks,

to march martial mullocks,

to see home. With all flocks.

IN LATE ZEAL

Terah brought his fortune

with ten thousand shekels,

quickly bought a chapel

with myriad acres;

requested his future

with the best of cupels

to golden grim statues

with the zest of pupils.

Instead of Chief Supremes,

praised his forge, fire pits,

daily sought rufous grids,

reddish bronze figurines,

core irons and wrought steel,

prisoned truth in late zeal,

yore icons and false seals,

poisoned troth in fake deals.

SWEETHOME

'Sweethome', gentility,

music and luxury,

sweetheart, fertility,

Abram and family

with gardeners gladly,

with handmaidens dearly,

with master chefs gaily

embraced Terah daily.

One shook warm hands strongly,

one washed worn feet humbly,

one sang sweet songs softly,

one lent lush lips lively:

smooth lyre melodies,

guests of delegacies,

sincere courtesies

blessed all delicacies.

BIRTH AND DEATH

Abram joyed little Lot,
Haran's boy, the newborn,
overjoyed kinfolk's soul
hundredfold was reborn.
Yet Nemrut remained cold,
in vengeance manyfold,
at manhunt with backsword,
disdained for young and old.

But brother and brother

did smell the rank order,

fought shoulder-to-shoulder

death spell of the odour.

Flagrant Flame's harsh hunger

hailed Haran's vague venture,

poignant pain's sheer shiver,

slow slaughter's vogue vulture.

EVER - PATHGUARD

Nannar with grim Ningal
to tease rascal vanguard,
thought less of grown Abram
as their ever-pathguard.
"We want faithful action,
fierce fight and attention,
with all satisfaction
stern strife and affection!"

Sole God, The Lone Constant,

to please Future Vanguard,

thought more of grown Abram

as his Ever-Pathguard.

"I wish faithful action,

his ease and attention,

with all satisfaction

his peace and affection!"

COVENANTS

ZIGGURAT

Enormous Ziggurat,

the utmost endeavour,

was Moongods' prime asset,

the upmost, the splendour;

blessed forestairs of haven

were praying low and deep,

leading stairs to Heaven,

parading more and steep.

Upon the long voyage
front steps of privilege,
along the lone passage
met stairs of pilgrimage;
as foremost sentinels
vigorous with prestige,
as topmost colonels
rigorous for the siege.

GRAND MASTER

And Abram with ambers

of moon-lifted levels,

enlightened by ambles

of star-gifted revels,

as a tablet writer,

as a harvest teller,

as a prudent scholar,

was called, "Dearest Master."

Amongst cheerful colours,

cumulated clusters,

amidst mirthful measures,

prolongated pleasures,

as an astrologer,

as an all-star-gazer,

as an astronomer

replied, "It's the Deemer!"

ELEGY

Synergy was flowing

at devotees' writhing.

elegy was growing

at coyotes' crying.

Song-fed winds were blowing

at lustral drums' beating.

bone-fed flames were glowing

at feral flutes' screaming.

Stoked feelings kept fading,
sinful fornicating,
what were needs acclaiming,
stenchful penetrating?
Smoked ceilings were aging,
presently degrading,
what were deeds proclaiming,
pleasantly disgracing?

APPETITE

Odd answer for asking
was Moongods' appetite
with hunger forewarning
high altar's ample size;
gold torches were flaming
followers' dim delight,
sore tortures were feeding
hallowers' seething sigh.

Procession was forming
serpentine of torchlights,
bald vultures were circling
scarlet sky for more thighs;
dusk maidens dropped on knees
down by the dread shrine,
daunting dreams and pleas
drowned in the red shine.

SARAI

Far gone was the fear

at Moonfeast's Leap Year.

Abram stared with pleasure

at Sarai's slim figure.

at her soul, the cleanest,

distantly related.

at her heart, the clearest,

instantly defeated.

at eyebeams of twinkles,

at lashes of sparkles,

at diadem of kiss curls,

at blushes of smiles,

at eyeglance of Princess,

at eyewinks of 'Goddess',

at vibrance of gladness

admitting their madness.

HAPPY FIRELILY

Happy Firelily

lavender, rosemary,

scentful jasmine, daisy

sweetly kept rose merry,

hungry hearts hopefully

shined the skies faithfully,

sunny souls mindfully

smiled in eyes fatefully,

as rosebuds addressing

the lovers, approaching.

as senses affecting

the echoes, applauding.

as feelings attracting

the glad cheeks, attacking.

as blessings attesting

the red lips, attaching.

RAPTURE

They tweeted with chuckles

at sunset of Sumer,

"My Sweetheart!, My Lover!"

enjoying the summer;

strolling streets together

light-hearted with fever,

looking at each other

true-hearted forever.

Olden engagement rings
revealed permanent feelings,
goldened coherent strings
rejoiced eminent darlings;
requited caressing
captured understanding,
excited embracing
raptured. Outstanding.

COVENANT OF LOVE

Sarai sang with Abram

of cherished good old days,

love stellar Inanna

and lavish cuddled faith,

as gleeful man and wife

swore emotion and lust,

at blissful grassland's shrine

warm devotion and trust.

"By Covenant's Letter

we belong together,

as caring doves nestle

we comfort each other,

to have Sons as Brothers,

Thriving Flock that Matters,

to share Hope and Altars,

Guiding God that Betters!" ...

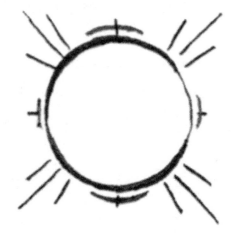

ENDNOTES

Page 12 - 13; ABRAHAM:

Avraham Avinu: /ahv-rah-HAHM ah-VEE-noo, אברהם אבינו / The Hebrew "Our father Abraham". In Judaism, he is the forefather of all Jews and the first believer of Yahweh (God).

Abraham: The father of monotheism (the belief in one supreme being), and of Abrahamic religions (Judaism, Christianity, Islam, and Bahá'í Faith) by his sons. Appears in the Hebrew Bible's (Tanakh's) Book of Genesis and in the Quran.

Onegod: Author's term for God.

Ibrahim, al-Khalil: Arabic "Abraham, a friend of Allah" (خليل الله). In Islam ~ is considered the link in the chain of prophets that begins with Adam and culminates in Muhammad.

Cradleland: The birthplace(s) of Abram (author).

Patriarch: In Greek "father of a family". In Christianity and Bahá'í Faith, Abraham is the progenitor of all believers.

Holyland: The land, Abraham got to (by the author).

Good Foothold: The Promised Land (by the author).

Page 14; THE CRY:

Ur: (/ʊr/; Sumerian Urim; Akkadian Uru; Arabic أُور; Hebrew אוּר) A Mesopotamian city-state from c. 3,800 BCE, which became dominant c.2,600 BCE at the mouth of the Euphrates on the Persian Gulf. Its ruins are part of the UNESCO World Heritage and lie well inland at Tell ell Muqayyar, Iraq.

Amathlai: Abram's mother, Terah's wife, is mentioned by name in the Talmudic sages, but not in the Book of Gen.

Floodland: Author's term for Mesopotamia (Greek '[land] between rivers'; calque of Akkadian *birit narim*), spanning modern-day Kuwait, Iraq, west Iran, south Turkey and Syria.

Terah (Hebrew: תֶּרַח): Father of Abram named in Genesis. Muslims maintain that Abra(ha)m's father is Azar.

Abram: ("Exalted father"). The "Earlz" name of Abraham

Page 16; CARING ONES:

Urudu: River Euphrates (/juːˈfreɪtiːz/) (Sumerian *burudu* "copper"; Arabic الفرات *al-Furāt*) originates in Turkey and flows through Syria and Iraq to join the Tigris. It was the main "route" for shipping copper ore.

Idigna: River Tigris (Sumerian "Swift river", Akkadian Idiqlat; Aramaic Diglat; Syriac Deqlat; Arabic دجل Dicle, Greek Τίγρις, Persian Tigrā), flows through the Armenian and Turkish Highlands, Syria, Iraq, and empties to the Persian Gulf.

Page 21; TERRACED FIRELILY:

Sumer: The first civilization (c.6,000 BCE, Copper Age) in southern Mesopotamia. The origin of the Akkadian word *šumerû* is uncertain. Sumerians called their land 'the Country of the noble lords' "*k-en-gi(-r)*" and their language "*Emegi(r)*". King Shulgi (2094-2046 BCE) described himself as "the king of the four quarters, the pastor of the black-headed people."

Page 24 - 25; HEADING HOME:

Harran: A southeastern Turkish town, founded by Sumerian traders from Ur dedicated to t h e Moon God (Nannar (2,500 BCE). (*Harrānu(m)* "journey, crossroad", חָרָן in Hebrew, حَرَّان in Arabic). Famous for its unique 'beehive' houses, history, and as hometown of Abram and his mother 'Amila'.

Nahor (I.): (Hebrew: נָחוֹר, *Nāḥōr*; Greek: Ναχώρ *Nakhór*) Son of Serug, father of Terah, grandfather of Abraham (Gen.11).

Nanna(r): Sumerian Moon God (Akk.: *EN.ZU*).

Hollow: Author's term for an open-air ritual place.

Page 26; GREAT LINEAGE:

Adam: The name given in Gen. 1-5 to the first human and patriarch, individually meaning "human" and in the collective sense "mankind". Gen. 1 explains God's creation of the world, while Gen. 2 the creation of Adam, the first man.

Eve: (/ˈiːv/) means "source of life"; "ḥāyâ","to live". She is the first woman and Adam'swife. Gen. 2 narrates how Eve was created, while Gen. 3 tells why Eveand Adam were expelled from the Garden of Eden and became immortal.

Page 26; GREAT LINEAGE continued:

Noah (/ˈnoʊ./): Lamech's son, the tenth and final of the pre-flood patriarchs. With a flood, God destroys the Earth, but helps Noah to save his family, mankind and land animals in his ark.

Shem: The son of Noah, father of Elam, Ashur, Lud, Aram and Arpachshad (Abraham's ancestor). The word "Semites" (former West Asians) derives from his name.

Page 36; CHASE OF DESIRE:

Belly Mound: Author's term for Göbekli Tepe (Turkish 'Potbelly Hill'; Kurdish: *Girê Mirazan*). It a UNESCO World Heritage site in Turkey. It's large circular communal structures and T-shaped st's one pillars with mostly animal decorations. It is the oldest known permanent settlement (c.9,500 BCE; Stone Age) of hunter-gatherers; "The birthplace of agriculture".

Page 39; SORROW:

Hammurabi: (/ˌxæmʊˈrɑːbi/. King of the Old Babylonian Empire (c.1,792-1,750 BCE), taking Mesopotamia under Babylonian rule. He is best known for his Code of Laws.

Babylon: (Old Babylonian: Bābilim, "gate of the god(s)"; Babylonian: Bab-ilu; Hebrew: Babel; Arabic: Atlal Bābil), known from c.2217 BCE with a natural ford on the Euphrates. As the cultural and political center of the Babylonian Empire, became the first city to reach a population of 200,000. Marduk (Sumerian: *amar utu.k* "bull-calf of the sun") was its patron deity. UNESCO World Heritage situated in Hillah, Babil, Iraq.

Page 42 - 43; FLOURISHED:

Nuna: Nickname for Amathlai by the author.

Nahor (II) and **Haran:** Sons of Nahor (I), appear in Genesis. The word *Nahor* relates to the root חרר(*harar*), to be a central hub of heat, and the word *Haran*, meaning "mountaineer".

Page 45; TIGHT BINDINGS:

Ningal: Sumerian Moon-goddess ("Great Queen"; Akkadian:Nikkal; "Lady" or "mother") and wife of Nannar.

Page 48 - 49; AGAINST ALL ODDS:
Idols: Abram breaks ~ in Genesis Rabbah (chapter 38).
Nemrut: Lgendary King Nimrod, "the mighty hunter" *Gen.10).. Two mountains are named after him (in Turkey) .
In Bahá'í Faith Nimrod "dreamed a dream", a new star.

Page 50 - 51; POWER OF FAITH:
Urfa: (Şanlıurfa "to bring water") A Turkish city near Göbekli Tepe. Nuna' gave birth to Abram in the local cave (part of Mosque of Mavlid-il-Halil Camii). Quran narrates Abram**'s** fight with Nemrutl. It **is** nicknamed "the City of Prophets".

Page 54; MARCHINGS:
Father's honour: Author's phrase for King Sin-Muballit.

Page 56; IN LATE ZEAL:
Shekel: (Akk. "weighing") A unit of weight, later a currency.

Page 58 - 59; SWEETHOME:
Sweethome: The House of Abraham located in Ur.
Lyres of Ur date back to c.2,500 BCE.

Page 60; BIRTH AND DEATH:
Lot: (Hebrew: לוֹט; "veil, covering". Son of Haran (Gen.).

Page 66; ZIGGURAT:
Ziggurat (Akk. "pinnacle") of Ur: A four-level, square structure with a top shrine (2,100 BCE) dedicated to Nannar.

Page 74; SARAI:
Sarai: (later Sarah, "princess," Old Hebrew: שָׂרָה; Arabic: رة سا Sārah; akkadian sharratu "queen").. Wife of Abra(ha)m.

Page 80; COVENANT OF LOVE:
Inanna: (Sum. "Lady of Heaven"; Ishtar (Akk.) Goddess of love, war, and fertility, associated with beauty, sex, divine law and power. Her parents are Nannar and Ningal. She appears in the *Epic of Gilgamesh* and in the *Sumerian Temple Hymn.*

Printed in Great Britain
by Amazon

36352984R00057